STEPHANIE MILLER

Nashville Tennessee Hot Spots and Hidden Gems

Discover all of the Top Attractions, Actvities and Restaurants to explore in Nashville Tennessee

Copyright © 2024 by Stephanie Miller

All rights reserved. No part of this publication may be reproduced, stored or transmitted in any form or by any means, electronic, mechanical, photocopying, recording, scanning, or otherwise without written permission from the publisher. It is illegal to copy this book, post it to a website, or distribute it by any other means without permission.

Stephanie Miller asserts the moral right to be identified as the author of this work.

Stephanie Miller has no responsibility for the persistence or accuracy of URLs for external or third-party Internet Websites referred to in this publication and does not guarantee that any content on such Websites is, or will remain, accurate or appropriate.

Designations used by companies to distinguish their products are often claimed as trademarks. All brand names and product names used in this book and on its cover are trade names, service marks, trademarks and registered trademarks of their respective owners. The publishers and the book are not associated with any product or vendor mentioned in this book. None of the companies referenced within the book have endorsed the book.

First edition

This book was professionally ty
Find out more o

Contents

Introduction	1
Harmony Along the Cumberland	2
Nashville's Hot Spots: A Guide to Unforgettable Experiences...	3
Historic and Entertaining Tours Through Nashville	7
Culinary Delights in Nashville	10
Nashville's Natural Treasures	13
The Sporting Pulse of Nashville	17
Nashville Family Adventures	20
Day Trips Beyond Nashville	23
Unveiling Nashville's Hidden Gems	26
Harmony in Music Valley	34
Conclusion	37
Resources	39

Introduction

Welcome to the Nashville Tennessee travel guide! My name is Stephanie Miller, and I'm extremely excited to be writing this book and sharing my favorite things about Music City USA. This will be a great resource for me to share with those who are always asking for suggestions when visiting Tennessee. I'm always excited when friends are planning a trip here and I hope they love it as much as I do. This condensed version will give you some must do's and highlights of the area that can't be missed.

My journey to Nashville…my dad is a cowboy. Growing up in the mountains, listening to country music in a small town in North Idaho is how I was introduced to country music and how it got into my blood. As an adult I traveled a bit and Nashville was always on my list of places that I wanted to visit. So 1 day I bought a plane ticket and headed off for a week to "check it out". I fell in love and 6 months later, I moved here. Nashville will always hold a special place in my heart and I am thrilled to be sharing it with you.

This handy little guide doesn't have every detail, but will definitely give you my top recommendations. So, let's get to it!

Harmony Along the Cumberland

Nestled along the winding banks of the Cumberland River, Nashville, Tennessee, has woven a rich tapestry of history that harmonizes cultural, musical, and political threads. The city's origins trace back to the late 18th century when it was established as Fort Nashborough by James Robertson and John Donelson. This outpost became a beacon for pioneers, and its settlement grew into a bustling community.

In the 19th century, Nashville flourished as a key transportation hub, connecting river commerce with emerging railroads. The city's strategic location during the Civil War earned it the nickname the "Athens of the South" for its cultural and educational institutions.

However, it was in the 20th century that Nashville solidified its status as the "Music City." The birthplace of country music, it became home to the Grand Ole Opry and the Country Music Hall of Fame, attracting musicians and fans worldwide. Nashville's musical tapestry expanded beyond country, embracing diverse genres like blues, rock, and gospel.

Today, the city stands as a testament to its resilient past, where history, music, and culture converge. From the historic streets of Germantown to the vibrant energy of Broadway, Nashville continues to sing its unique tune, inviting visitors to step into the rhythm of its storied history.

Nashville's Hot Spots: A Guide to Unforgettable Experiences in Music City"

Nashville, Tennessee, the heart of country music, is a city that resonates with the twang of guitars and the soulful tunes of yesteryear. From the iconic Grand Ole Opry to the historic Ryman Auditorium, and the sprawling halls of the Country Music Hall of Fame, Nashville offers a symphony of experiences for music enthusiasts and history buffs alike. In this chapter, we'll explore the top 10 things to do in Music City, with each attraction contributing to the rich tapestry of Nashville's cultural heritage.

Grand Ole Opry: The Soul of Nashville
- Established in 1925, the Grand Ole Opry is a living legend in the world of country music.
- Experience the magic of live radio broadcasts and witness performances from legendary and emerging country artists.
- Take a backstage tour to discover the Opry's storied history, with its iconic wooden circle that was transported from the original Ryman Auditorium.

Ryman Auditorium: The Mother Church of Country Music
- Attend a live performance and immerse yourself in the intimate and acoustically superb atmosphere that has hosted legends like Johnny

Cash and Dolly Parton.

●Explore the Ryman's captivating exhibits, which showcase its evolution from a religious venue to a musical mecca.

Country Music Hall of Fame: Where Legends Live Forever

●Delve into the history of country music at the Country Music Hall of Fame, home to the genre's most cherished artifacts and memorabilia.

●Discover exhibits highlighting the careers of iconic artists and songwriters, including Hank Williams, Patsy Cline, and Merle Haggard.

●Engage in interactive displays, recording booths, and educational programs that celebrate the evolution of country music.

Honky Tonk Highway: Nashville's Neon-lit Entertainment Strip

●Take a stroll down Lower Broadway, famously known as the Honky Tonk Highway, where neon lights and live music spill out of every bar.

●Immerse yourself in the lively atmosphere of iconic honky-tonks like Tootsie's Orchid Lounge and Robert's Western World.

●Enjoy live performances from talented local musicians and experience the vibrant energy that defines Nashville's nightlife.

Parthenon: A Touch of Greece in the South

●Explore Centennial Park and marvel at the full-scale replica of the Parthenon, a testament to Nashville's nickname, the "Athens of the South."

●Admire the impressive statue of Athena inside the Parthenon and wander through the art gallery showcasing American paintings from the 19th and 20th centuries.

Johnny Cash Museum: A Tribute to The Man in Black

●Pay homage to the legendary Johnny Cash at the museum dedicated to his life and career.

●View rare artifacts, costumes, and personal items belonging to the

Man in Black.
● Immerse yourself in Cash's journey through engaging exhibits and multimedia displays, providing insight into his lasting impact on the music industry.

Music Row: Where Hits Are Made
● Take a walking tour of Music Row, the heartbeat of Nashville's music industry.
● Visit historic recording studios and witness the creative process that has produced countless hits.
● Marvel at the significance of this neighborhood in shaping the careers of iconic artists and songwriters.

Opryland Hotel: A Resort Oasis in the Heart of Nashville
● Step into the grandeur of Gaylord Opryland Resort, an expansive hotel and entertainment complex.
● Stroll through lush gardens, cascading waterfalls, and indoor atriums that create a serene escape.
● Catch a live performance or dine in one of the resort's fine restaurants for a luxurious experience.

Bicentennial Capitol Mall: A Walk Through History
● Explore Bicentennial Capitol Mall State Park, a tribute to Tennessee's 200 years of statehood.
● Wander through the various landmarks, including the World War II Memorial and the Court of 3 Stars, representing the three grand divisions of Tennessee.
● Learn about the state's history through informative plaques, statues, and the interactive Wall of History.

Nashville is a city that harmonizes its musical roots with a deep appreciation for history and culture. From the hallowed grounds of the Grand Ole Opry to the modern allure of the Opryland Hotel, each attraction contributes to the city's unique identity. Whether you're a country music enthusiast, a history buff, or simply a traveler seeking vibrant experiences, Nashville offers a symphony of delights that will leave an indelible mark on your heart and soul

Historic and Entertaining Tours Through Nashville

Nashville, often referred to as "Music City," is a city rich in history and culture. In this chapter, we'll explore some of the most iconic tours and attractions that showcase the city's diverse heritage and vibrant entertainment scene.

Cheekwood: A Symphony of Art and Nature
- Nestled on 55 acres of breathtaking gardens and grounds, Cheekwood offers visitors a unique blend of art and nature.
- Explore the historic Cheekwood Mansion, adorned with stunning art collections and surrounded by botanical gardens that change with the seasons.
- Don't miss the rotating exhibits in the museum, highlighting both local and international artists.

Belle Meade Plantation: A Stroll Through Antebellum Elegance
- Step back in time as you visit Belle Meade Plantation, an 1853 Greek Revival mansion known for its thoroughbred racing heritage.
- Take a guided tour through the mansion and its beautifully preserved outbuildings, gaining insight into the plantation's fascinating history.
- Learn about the impact of African American slaves and their

contributions to the plantation's success.

The Hermitage: Home of President Andrew Jackson
- Delve into the life of the seventh President of the United States by visiting The Hermitage, Andrew Jackson's historic estate.
- Tour the mansion, explore the beautiful gardens, and gain a deeper understanding of Jackson's legacy.
- Participate in educational programs that shed light on the complexities of the time, including discussions on slavery and Native American relations.

Belmont Mansion: A Glimpse into Victorian Opulence
- Experience the grandeur of Belmont Mansion, a stunning 19th-century home that once belonged to Adelicia Acklen, a prominent Nashville socialite.
- Marvel at the architecture and interior design reflecting the opulence of the Victorian era.
- Learn about the fascinating life of Adelicia Acklen, who played a significant role in shaping Nashville's cultural landscape.

Civil War History: Lotz House, Carter House, and Carnton House
- Immerse yourself in the poignant history of the Civil War by visiting three significant sites.
- Lotz House: Explore the Civil War narrative through the eyes of a German immigrant family at Lotz House, known for its compelling stories and well-preserved artifacts.
- Carter House: Step onto the battlefield where the Battle of Franklin unfolded, and tour the Carter House to witness the impact of the war on this historic home.
- Carnton House: Visit the Carnton House, a plantation turned field hospital during the war, and learn about the resilience of the people

who lived through these challenging times.

Home of the Stars: A Glimpse into Celebrity Residences
●Take a guided tour through the neighborhoods of Nashville where many country music stars call home.
●Get a closer look at the residences of iconic musicians, gaining insight into the city's role in the music industry.

Redneck Comedy Club: Laughter in Music City
●Unwind and enjoy a night of laughter at the Redneck Comedy Club, a popular venue known for its hilarious stand-up acts.
●Experience the unique brand of humor that combines Southern charm with comedic storytelling.

Nashville's tours provide a dynamic blend of history, culture, and entertainment, offering visitors a comprehensive experience that reflects the city's vibrant spirit. Whether exploring historic mansions or enjoying a night of comedy, Music City has something for everyone.

Culinary Delights in Nashville

Nashville, Tennessee, is not only renowned for its vibrant music scene but also boasts a burgeoning culinary landscape that caters to diverse tastes. From traditional Southern comfort food to innovative international flavors, the city has something to offer every palate. Here, we present a curated list of the top 10 restaurants in Nashville, considering both their gastronomic excellence and affordability.

Hattie B's Hot Chicken ($)
Location: 5209 Charlotte Ave, Nashville, TN 37209
Known for its iconic hot chicken, Hattie B's is a must-visit for spice enthusiasts. The menu features various heat levels, allowing patrons to customize their chicken experience. The casual atmosphere and wallet-friendly prices make it a local favorite.

Arnold's Country Kitchen ($$)
Location: 605 8th Ave S, Nashville, TN 37203
Arnold's Country Kitchen is a Nashville institution, serving traditional "meat and three" Southern fare. The rotating daily menu offers a selection of meats and hearty sides, providing a true taste of Tennessee's culinary heritage.

Prince's Hot Chicken Shack ($$)

Location: 123 Ewing Dr, Nashville, TN 37207
Another hotspot for hot chicken, Prince's is a local legend. The no-frills joint serves up fiery chicken that has gained national acclaim. Prepare for a flavor-packed experience in a casual setting.

Rolf and Daughters ($$$)
Location: 700 Taylor St, Nashville, TN 37208
For those seeking a more refined dining experience, Rolf and Daughters offers a contemporary take on Southern and Italian-inspired cuisine. The industrial-chic atmosphere complements the inventive dishes prepared with locally sourced ingredients.

Edley's Bar-B-Que ($)
Location: 908 Main St, Nashville, TN 37206
Edley's Bar-B-Que is a barbecue lover's paradise. With a laid-back vibe and a menu featuring smoked meats, classic sides, and inventive sandwiches, this spot captures the essence of Tennessee barbecue.

The Catbird Seat ($$$$)
Location: 1711 Division St, Nashville, TN 37203
For an unparalleled culinary experience, The Catbird Seat offers a chef-driven tasting menu in an intimate setting. The innovative dishes and open kitchen concept provide a unique and memorable dining adventure.

Peg Leg Porker ($$)
Location: 903 Gleaves St, Nashville, TN 37203
Specializing in Tennessee-style barbecue, Peg Leg Porker is a favorite among locals. The dry-rubbed ribs and pulled pork showcase the rich barbecue heritage of the region.

Bartaco ($$)

Location: 2526 12th Ave S, Nashville, TN 37204

For a taste of coastal-inspired cuisine, Bartaco offers a diverse menu of tacos, rice bowls, and small plates. The beachy ambiance and fresh flavors make it a popular spot for casual dining.

Mas Tacos Por Favor ($)

Location: 732 Mcferrin Ave, Nashville, TN 37206

Embracing a laid-back atmosphere, Mas Tacos Por Favor serves authentic Mexican street food. The affordable prices and flavorful dishes attract both locals and visitors alike.

Monell's Dining & Catering ($$)

Location: 1235 6th Ave N, Nashville, TN 37208

If you're craving a communal dining experience, Monell's is the place to go. This family-style restaurant serves hearty Southern meals, encouraging patrons to pass dishes around the table and share in the joy of good food.

As you explore the culinary delights of Nashville, these top 12 restaurants offer a diverse range of flavors, atmospheres, and price points, ensuring that every dining experience is a memorable one. Whether you're a local or a visitor, these establishments capture the essence of Nashville's thriving food scene.

Nashville's Natural Treasures

Nashville, often referred to as the "Music City," isn't just about the beats and melodies that echo through its vibrant streets. The city boasts a rich tapestry of natural wonders, offering residents and visitors alike a chance to escape the urban hustle and immerse themselves in the serene beauty of its parks. In this chapter, we'll explore some of Nashville's most iconic green spaces, each with its unique charm and allure.

Centennial Park

Nestled in the heart of Nashville, Centennial Park is a verdant oasis that spans 132 acres, providing a breath of fresh air amid the city's lively atmosphere. Here, visitors can discover a blend of recreational activities, historical landmarks, and artistic inspirations.

● The Parthenon: Dominating the landscape is a full-scale replica of the Parthenon, a testament to Nashville's nickname as the "Athens of the South." Tourists and locals alike marvel at the grandeur of this ancient Greek temple, which serves as both an art museum and a nod to the city's cultural heritage.

● Lake Watauga: Centennial Park's centerpiece, Lake Watauga, invites visitors to stroll along its tranquil shores or rent paddleboats for a leisurely afternoon on the water. The reflections of the surrounding greenery create a picturesque scene that contrasts with the urban skyline.

● Events and Festivals: Throughout the year, Centennial Park hosts a myriad of events and festivals, from live music concerts to art exhibits. The park becomes a hub of cultural activity, uniting the community in celebration.

Tennessee State Capitol Park

Steeped in history, Tennessee State Capitol Park stands as a testament to the state's political legacy. This park, situated on the grounds surrounding the Tennessee State Capitol, provides a serene setting for reflection and relaxation.

● War Memorials: The park is adorned with various war memorials, honoring the sacrifices of those who served in conflicts throughout history. Each monument tells a story of bravery and resilience, reminding visitors of the importance of freedom and unity.

● Landscaped Gardens: Immaculately landscaped gardens surround the Capitol, offering a peaceful escape for those seeking solace amid blooming flowers and carefully manicured greenery.

● Bicentennial Mall: Adjacent to the park, the Bicentennial Mall invites exploration with its informative exhibits and walking trails. Visitors can learn about Tennessee's rich history and cultural heritage while enjoying the open-air museum.

Warner Parks

For nature enthusiasts, Warner Parks, comprising Percy Warner Park and Edwin Warner Park, beckon with sprawling woodlands and diverse ecosystems. These interconnected parks provide a haven for outdoor activities and wildlife exploration.

● Hiking Trails: Miles of hiking trails wind through the parks, offering hikers a chance to connect with nature and discover hidden waterfalls, scenic overlooks, and a variety of plant and animal species.

● Equestrian Trails: Percy Warner Park, in particular, boasts equestrian trails, allowing horseback riders to traverse the picturesque landscapes. The rhythmic clip-clop of hooves provides a unique and nostalgic ambiance.

● Nature Center: The Warner Parks Nature Center serves as an educational hub, providing programs and exhibits that deepen visitors' understanding of the region's flora and fauna. It's a valuable resource for school groups, families, and curious individuals alike.

Radnor Lake

Nestled just a short drive from downtown Nashville, Radnor Lake State Park is a haven for wildlife enthusiasts and those seeking a peaceful escape. The park's centerpiece, Radnor Lake, reflects the tranquility of its surroundings.

● Wildlife Watching: Radnor Lake is renowned for its diverse birdlife, including migratory species that make seasonal stops at the park. Birdwatchers can spot herons, eagles, and a variety of waterfowl.

● No Motorized Boats: To preserve the serenity of the lake, only non-motorized boats are allowed. This restriction enhances the overall peacefulness, creating an ideal environment for kayaking and paddleboarding.

● Educational Programs: The park offers educational programs that delve into the natural history of the area. Guided hikes, birding walks, and informative sessions enhance the visitor experience.

Shelby Bottoms

On the banks of the Cumberland River, Shelby Bottoms Greenway and Natural Area provide a scenic escape within the city limits. This expansive green space, characterized by wetlands, forests, and meadows, offers a diverse array of recreational opportunities.

● Biking Trails: With miles of paved and unpaved biking trails, Shelby Bottoms caters to cyclists of all skill levels. The flat terrain makes it accessible for both leisurely rides and more intense cycling adventures.

● Cumberland River Pedestrian Bridge: Connecting Shelby Bottoms to the Cumberland River Pedestrian Bridge, visitors can enjoy stunning views of the river and the Nashville skyline. It's a prime spot for sunset strolls and photography.

● Nature Center and Playground: Families can explore the Nature Center, which provides educational exhibits and hosts interactive programs. The adjacent playground offers a space for children to play and expend their energy.

Nashville's natural treasures, from the iconic Centennial Park to the peaceful Shelby Bottoms, showcase the city's commitment to providing accessible and diverse green spaces for its residents and guests. Each park tells a unique story, weaving together history, culture, and the beauty of the natural world. So, whether you seek a quiet refuge, an outdoor adventure, or a cultural experience, Nashville's parks offer a little something for everyone.

The Sporting Pulse of Nashville

Nashville, Tennessee, renowned for its vibrant music scene, is not just a melody of tunes; it is also a symphony of sports, echoing the passion and fervor of its residents. In this chapter, we delve into the diverse sports culture that thrives in the heart of the Volunteer State.

The Titans Roar
The Tennessee Titans, Nashville's pride in the NFL, create ripples of excitement across the city. Nissan Stadium, their home ground, transforms into a sea of navy blue and Titans gold on game days. The thunderous cheers of the fans resonate through the city, creating an atmosphere that's electric with anticipation and team spirit.

Smashville's Hockey Fever
The Nashville Predators, Nashville's professional ice hockey team, have turned the city into 'Smashville.' The Bridgestone Arena becomes a battleground for intense clashes on the ice. The iconic catfish toss tradition and the deafening chants of the Predators' loyal fan base make every game a spectacle, leaving an indelible mark on Nashville's sports landscape.

Sounds of Baseball
First Tennessee Park is the heartbeat of baseball in Nashville, hosting

the Nashville Sounds, the Triple-A affiliate of the Milwaukee Brewers. Families gather for a relaxing day at the ballpark, indulging in the timeless tradition of enjoying hot dogs and cheering for home runs under the summer sun.

Soccer's Southern Sojourn

The Nashville SC, the city's Major League Soccer team, has brought the beautiful game to Music City. The passionate supporters, known as The Roadies, paint the stadium in gold and blue, adding a touch of soccer fever to the eclectic sports scene in Nashville.

Racing at Fairgrounds Speedway

The Fairgrounds Speedway, with its rich history dating back to 1904, adds a dose of adrenaline to Nashville's sports portfolio. Racing enthusiasts gather to witness thrilling NASCAR events and feel the roar of engines at this iconic venue.

College Sports Extravaganza

Vanderbilt University, located in the heart of Nashville, contributes significantly to the city's sports narrative. From the Commodores' prowess on the football field to the exhilarating basketball games at Memorial Gymnasium, college sports are an integral part of Nashville's sports culture.

Music City Marathon

Beyond traditional sports, Nashville hosts the St. Jude Rock 'n' Roll Marathon, combining the city's love for running with its musical heritage. Thousands of runners pound the pavement, passing iconic landmarks and live music stages, creating a unique marathon experience that reflects the soul of Nashville.

Sports Bars and Fan Zones

Nashville's sports culture extends beyond the arenas to its numerous sports bars and fan zones. Whether it's catching a game with friends at a local pub on Broadway or joining fellow fans in the dedicated fan zones outside stadiums, the camaraderie among Nashvillians is palpable.

Nashville, a city synonymous with music, is also a haven for sports enthusiasts. From the roar of the Titans to the twang of hockey pucks in Smashville, Nashville's sports scene is as diverse and dynamic as its musical heritage. The city's sports culture is not just about the games; it's about the shared experiences, the traditions, and the indomitable spirit that unites Nashvillians in their love for sports.

Nashville Family Adventures

Once upon a time, in the lively city of Nashville, there were magical places that kids loved to explore. Let's embark on a journey through some of the most exciting spots that made children's hearts race with joy.

Nashville Zoo: A Wild Wonderland
- Nestled in the heart of Nashville, the Nashville Zoo is a paradise for animal lovers.
- Kids can meet their favorite furry, scaly, and feathery friends, from playful lemurs to majestic elephants.
- Don't miss the Kangaroo Kickabout, where you can hop alongside these bouncy creatures.
- The Jungle Gym provides a fantastic place for little ones to burn off energy while parents relax.

Adventure Science Center: Unleash Your Inner Scientist
- Step into a world of wonder and discovery at the Adventure Science Center.
- Explore hands-on exhibits that make science fun and engaging for kids of all ages.
- The Space Chase exhibit lets young astronauts explore the wonders of the universe.

- Science Live! shows bring STEM concepts to life with exciting experiments.

SoundWaves at Gaylord: Splash into Fun
- Dive into a world of aquatic excitement at SoundWaves, located at the Gaylord Opryland Resort.
- Enjoy thrilling water slides, a lazy river for a relaxing float, and a wave pool that makes every day feel like a beach day.
- The FlowRider is perfect for those aspiring young surfers looking to catch their first wave.
- After a day of water-filled adventures, unwind in the soothing warm waters of the adult-only pool.

Adventure Works: Conquer the Treetops
- For the little adventurers who love a challenge, Adventure Works is the place to be.
- Test your courage on the high ropes courses and zip lines that weave through the treetops.
- Safety is a top priority, and experienced guides ensure a thrilling yet secure experience.
- Kids can build confidence and teamwork skills while conquering obstacles high above the ground.

Nashville Shores: Lakeside Fun
- Head to the shores of Percy Priest Lake for a day of aquatic fun at Nashville Shores.
- Splash around in the massive water park featuring slides, wave pools, and a lazy river.
- The Treetop Adventure Park offers a thrilling aerial course for those seeking an adrenaline rush.
- Families can relax on the sandy beach, build sandcastles, and enjoy

picnics by the water.

Nashville, with its vibrant mix of wildlife, science wonders, water adventures, treetop challenges, and lakeside fun, is a treasure trove of excitement for kids of all ages. So, put on your explorer hats and get ready for a magical journey through the Music City's favorite haunts!

Day Trips Beyond Nashville

Nashville, the vibrant heart of Tennessee, offers more than just its iconic music scene. Venture beyond the city limits, and you'll discover a treasure trove of day trip destinations. Whether you're a history buff, a nature lover, or a connoisseur of spirits, there's something for everyone. Embark on a journey through the picturesque landscapes and rich cultural heritage surrounding Nashville.

Jack Daniel's Distillery (Approx. 70 miles south of Nashville):
● Immerse yourself in the world of Tennessee whiskey with a visit to the Jack Daniel's Distillery.
● Take a guided tour to witness the whiskey-making process and learn about the history of this iconic brand.
● Explore the charming town of Lynchburg, where the distillery is located, and savor Southern cuisine in local eateries.

Franklin Historic District (Approx. 20 miles south of Nashville):
● Step back in time as you wander through the historic streets of Franklin.
● Visit the Carter House and Carnton Plantation to gain insights into the Civil War history of the region.
● Explore boutiques, antique shops, and enjoy a meal at one of the many charming restaurants in the downtown area.

Natchez Trace Parkway (Access points within 20-50 miles from Nashville):
● Embark on a scenic drive along the Natchez Trace Parkway, a historic route connecting Nashville to Natchez, Mississippi.
● Stop at various points of interest, such as the historic Tobacco Farm and the iconic Double Arch Bridge for breathtaking views.
● Hike or bike along the numerous trails, immersing yourself in the beauty of the surrounding nature.

Arrington Vineyards (Approx. 30 miles south of Nashville):
● Indulge in a day of wine tasting at Arrington Vineyards, nestled in the rolling hills of Tennessee.
● Enjoy a picnic on the winery grounds while sampling a variety of locally produced wines.
● Take in the scenic views of the vineyards and make sure to catch live music events held regularly at the winery.

Bell Buckle (Approx. 60 miles southeast of Nashville):
● Experience small-town charm in Bell Buckle, known for its Victorian architecture and antique shops.
● Stroll down Railroad Square and visit the famous Bell Buckle Café for a taste of Southern comfort food.
● Don't miss the annual RC Cola and MoonPie Festival, celebrating the town's quirky history.

Mammoth Cave National Park (Approx. 85 miles northwest of Nashville):
● Venture into the underground wonders of Mammoth Cave, the world's longest known cave system.
● Choose from a variety of cave tours, ranging from easy walks to

challenging explorations.
- Explore the surface trails and enjoy the natural beauty of the park, making it a perfect destination for outdoor enthusiasts.

Burgess Falls State Park (Approx. 80 miles east of Nashville):
- Hike the scenic trails of Burgess Falls State Park, leading to stunning waterfalls.
- Witness the cascading waters of Burgess Falls, offering a picturesque backdrop for nature lovers and photographers.
- Pack a picnic and spend a day surrounded by the tranquility of the park.

Fall Creek Falls State Park (Approx. 130 miles east of Nashville):
- Discover the beauty of Tennessee's tallest waterfall at Fall Creek Falls State Park.
- Hike through lush forests, visit the nature center, and explore the park's various scenic overlooks.
- Engage in outdoor activities such as fishing, bird watching, and zip-lining for a day filled with adventure.

Escape the hustle and bustle of Nashville and embark on these enriching day trips, each offering a unique blend of history, nature, and culture. From the historic charm of Franklin to the natural wonders of Mammoth Cave, these destinations provide a diverse range of experiences, all within a comfortable distance from the lively city of Nashville.

Unveiling Nashville's Hidden Gems

Nashville, often celebrated as the heart of country music, is a city that pulsates with vibrant culture, rich history, and an array of hidden gems waiting to be discovered. Beyond the neon lights of Broadway and the twang of guitar strings, Nashville harbors lesser-known treasures that offer a unique and intimate experience for locals and visitors alike.

Bluebird Cafe

Location: 4104 Hillsboro Pike, Nashville, TN 37215

● Overview: Nestled in a strip mall, the Bluebird Cafe is an unassuming venue that has played a pivotal role in shaping the careers of renowned songwriters. With an intimate setting, it offers a chance to witness raw talent up close.

● Why Visit:

● Acoustic performances by both established and emerging songwriters.

● Intimate atmosphere, fostering a connection between performers and the audience.

● Reservations are highly recommended due to limited seating.

The Fontanel Mansion

Location: 4225 Whites Creek Pike, Whites Creek, TN 37189

● Overview: Once the residence of country legend Barbara Mandrell,

Fontanel has transformed into a unique entertainment complex with various attractions, including a mansion tour, ziplining, and live music events.
- Why Visit:
- Explore the opulent Mandrell Mansion and its lush surroundings.
- Ziplining adventure through the picturesque Fontanel grounds.
- Concerts featuring a mix of genres in the outdoor amphitheater.

Loveless Cafe

Location: 8400 TN-100, Nashville, TN 37221
- Overview: A timeless institution, Loveless Cafe is a haven for Southern comfort food enthusiasts. Famous for its biscuits and preserves, this roadside eatery has been a beloved stop for travelers since 1951.
- Why Visit:
- Indulge in a hearty Southern breakfast featuring the famous Loveless biscuits.
- Gift shop with an array of jams, jellies, and Southern-themed merchandise.
- Quaint cottages for those wanting an overnight stay in the charming surroundings.

RCA Studio B

Location: 1611 Roy Acuff Pl, Nashville, TN 37203
- Overview: Step into the birthplace of timeless hits recorded by Elvis Presley, Dolly Parton, and countless others. RCA Studio B, known as the "Home of a Thousand Hits," offers guided tours delving into the history of music production.
- Why Visit:
- Explore the legendary recording studio with a knowledgeable guide.

● Listen to anecdotes about the recording sessions that shaped the music industry.

● An opportunity to play the studio's historic piano.

Marathon Village

Location: 1305 Clinton St, Nashville, TN 37203

● Overview: Housed in a former automobile factory, Marathon Village is a historic complex that seamlessly blends art, shopping, and dining. Its red-brick walls tell tales of Nashville's industrial past.

● Why Visit:

● Eclectic mix of shops featuring local artists and craftsmen.

● Antique Archaeology, co-owned by Mike Wolfe of "American Pickers" fame, is a must-visit for vintage finds.

● Enjoy craft beer at the onsite Jackalope Brewing Company.

Vanderbilt Dyer Observatory

Location: 1000 Oman Dr, Brentwood, TN 37027

● Overview: Perched atop a hill, the Vanderbilt Dyer Observatory offers a celestial escape from the city lights. The observatory hosts public programs, stargazing events, and educational activities.

● Why Visit:

● Public telescope nights for observing planets, stars, and other celestial wonders.

● Engaging educational programs for both adults and children.

● Breathtaking views of the night sky away from urban light pollution.

Puckett's Restaurant

Location: Multiple locations, including 500 Church St, Nashville, TN 37219

● Overview: Puckett's is more than just a restaurant; it's a hub for live

music and Southern cuisine. With its roots in Leiper's Fork, Puckett's has expanded its reach while maintaining its commitment to local flavor and hospitality.
● Why Visit:
● Live music performances by local artists while enjoying a meal.
● Menu featuring Southern classics and creative twists on regional dishes.
● Rustic and welcoming ambiance, capturing the essence of Tennessee.

Lane Motor Museum
Location: 702 Murfreesboro Pike, Nashville, TN 37210
● Overview: Car enthusiasts and curious minds alike will find delight in the Lane Motor Museum. This offbeat museum houses a vast collection of unique and rare vehicles from around the world.
● Why Visit:
● Over 500 cars and motorcycles on display, ranging from the peculiar to the classic.
● A diverse array of vehicles, including microcars, amphibious cars, and one-of-a-kind prototypes.
● Interactive exhibits exploring the history and engineering of automobiles.

Assembly Food Hall
Location: 4th Avenue South & Broadway, Nashville, TN 37201
● Overview: Situated in the heart of downtown Nashville, Assembly Food Hall is a culinary haven with diverse dining options, from gourmet tacos to decadent desserts, all under one roof.
● Why Visit:
● A culinary adventure with a wide range of cuisines to choose from.
● Vibrant atmosphere with communal seating and live entertainment.

● Perfect for groups with diverse food preferences.

TPAC (Tennessee Performing Arts Center)

Location: 505 Deaderick St, Nashville, TN 37243

● Overview: TPAC stands as a cultural cornerstone, hosting Broadway shows, concerts, and performances that showcase the city's commitment to the arts.

● Why Visit:

● Broadway productions and touring performances in a state-of-the-art venue.

● Diverse range of cultural events, from ballet to stand-up comedy.

● Educational programs and community engagement initiatives.

Wild Beaver Saloon Location: 212 Commerce St, Nashville, TN 37201

● Overview: A lively honky-tonk with a twist, Wild Beaver Saloon adds a dash of rock 'n' roll to the traditional Nashville scene. With its energetic vibe and diverse playlist, it stands out among the bustling Broadway venues.

● Why Visit:

● Live music spanning various genres, including rock, pop, and country.

● Mechanical bull rides for those seeking an extra thrill.

● Unique atmosphere, blending the classic honky-tonk vibe with modern flair.

Nashville Symphony

Location: Schermerhorn Symphony Center, 1 Symphony Pl, Nashville, TN 37201

● Overview: The Grammy Award-winning Nashville Symphony enchants audiences with its world-class performances. The Schermerhorn Symphony Center, an architectural masterpiece, serves as its stunning

backdrop.
- Why Visit:
- Orchestra performances featuring classical, pops, and special guest artists.
- Acoustically superb venue with a visually striking design.
- Educational programs, including free community concerts and music education initiatives.

Nashville Farmers' Market
Location: 900 Rosa L Parks Blvd, Nashville, TN 37208
- Overview: A bustling hub of local agriculture, the Nashville Farmers' Market offers an immersive experience where visitors can savor fresh produce, artisanal goods, and diverse culinary offerings.
- Why Visit:
- Farm sheds featuring a variety of fresh produce, meats, and handmade products.
- International Market House with global cuisine from various cultures.
- Special events, workshops, and cooking classes for an enriching experience.

Union Station Hotel
Location: 1001 Broadway, Nashville, TN 37203
- Overview: Immerse yourself in the grandeur of Nashville's history by staying at the Union Station Hotel. This opulent hotel, once a bustling train station, seamlessly blends timeless elegance with modern luxury.
- Why Visit:
- Architectural splendor with stunning arched windows, chandeliers, and intricate details.
- Unique rooms and suites that showcase the building's historic

character.

- Prime location, offering easy access to downtown attractions and entertainment.

Biscuit Love

Location: 316 11th Ave S, Nashville, TN 37203

- Overview: Biscuit Love has become a breakfast sensation, drawing crowds with its delectable biscuit-based dishes. From sweet to savory, the menu celebrates the beloved biscuit in all its glory.
- Why Visit:
- Signature dishes like the Bonuts (fried biscuit dough with lemon mascarpone and blueberry compote).
- Southern-inspired breakfast and brunch menu with a modern twist.
- Cozy ambiance and friendly service, creating a welcoming breakfast haven.

Grilled Cheeserie

Location: 2003 Belcourt Ave, Nashville, TN 37212

- Overview: Elevating the humble grilled cheese sandwich to gourmet heights, Grilled Cheeserie is a food truck turned brick-and-mortar restaurant. It caters to both traditionalists and adventurous eaters with its creative twists on the classic comfort food.
- Why Visit:
- Gourmet grilled cheese sandwiches featuring high-quality, locally sourced ingredients.
- Seasonal specials and rotating menu options for variety.
- Food truck nostalgia with the convenience of a dedicated location.

Nashville's hidden gems beckon those willing to venture off the beaten path, offering a tapestry of experiences that go beyond the city's renowned music scene. From the iconic Bluebird Cafe to the astronomical wonders at Vanderbilt Dyer Observatory, each hidden gem adds a unique thread to the vibrant fabric of Music City. As you explore these diverse attractions, you'll discover the soul of Nashville, a city that harmonizes tradition and innovation, creating an unforgettable journey for all who seek its treasures.

Harmony in Music Valley

Nestled within the heart of Nashville, Music Valley emerges as a vibrant tapestry of musical history, entertainment, and cultural landmarks. As the sun sets, the neon lights come alive, illuminating a haven for music enthusiasts and curious wanderers alike.

Nestled within the heart of Nashville, Music Valley emerges as a vibrant tapestry of musical history, entertainment, and cultural landmarks. As the sun sets, the neon lights come alive, illuminating a haven for music enthusiasts and curious wanderers alike.

Nashville Palace: A Honky-Tonk Gem
   The Nashville Palace, a legendary honky-tonk, stands as a living testament to the city's rich country music heritage. With its rustic charm and live performances, it's a must-visit for those seeking an authentic Nashville experience.

Cooters Museum: A Dash of Dukes of Hazzard
   Step into the Cooters Museum, a nostalgic tribute to "The Dukes of Hazzard." Explore memorabilia, costumes, and the iconic General Lee car, bringing the beloved TV show to life.

Willie Nelson's Legacy at the Texas Troubadour Theater

The Texas Troubadour Theater echoes with the soulful tunes and legacy of Willie Nelson. A haven for country music aficionados, this venue hosts live performances, paying homage to the legendary "Red Headed Stranger."

Nashville Nightlife Theater: A Symphony of Lights
Venture into the Nashville Nightlife Theater, where the city's musical pulse beats strongest. Live performances, spanning genres from country to blues, create a symphony of lights and sounds that captivate audiences.

Midnight Jamboree: Keeping the Tradition Alive
The Midnight Jamboree, a radio show dating back to 1947, continues to broadcast live from the Texas Troubadour Theater. Immerse yourself in the timeless tunes that have graced the airwaves for decades.

Cowboy Church: A Spiritual Note in Music Valley
Find solace and spirituality at the Cowboy Church, where the twang of guitars mixes with the hymns, creating a unique worship experience rooted in Nashville's musical roots.

Music City Bar and Grill: A Melodic Fusion
The Music City Bar and Grill offers a melodic fusion of live music, delicious food, and a lively atmosphere. This venue is a hotspot for locals and tourists alike, seeking the perfect blend of southern hospitality and musical entertainment.

Scoreboards: Where Sports and Music Converge
For sports enthusiasts seeking a musical twist, Scoreboards provides the perfect harmony. Catch a game while enjoying live music, creating an atmosphere where sports and music coexist seamlessly.

Madame Tussauds Nashville: Waxing Poetic with Music Icons

Madame Tussauds Nashville invites you to get up close and personal with lifelike wax figures of music legends. Walk among the stars, from Johnny Cash to Dolly Parton, capturing the essence of Music City's iconic personalities.

As you wander through Music Valley, each note, each venue, and each experience contribute to the symphony that is Nashville's soul – a place where music and culture intertwine in perfect harmony

Conclusion

In concluding this exploration of Nashville, Tennessee's vibrant hot spots and hidden gems, it is evident that the city's allure extends far beyond its musical roots. From the pulsating rhythms of Lower Broadway to the serene landscapes along the Cumberland River, Nashville reveals a multifaceted tapestry of culture, history, and contemporary charm.

The hot spots, with their neon-lit honky-tonks and energetic crowds, epitomize the city's musical heartbeat. Each venue carries the weight of Nashville's legendary music legacy, echoing the footsteps of icons who once graced its stages. Yet, as we ventured into the hidden gems, a different narrative unfolded — one of intimate cafes, tucked-away galleries, and overlooked historical gems. These treasures breathe life into the city's diverse character, offering a respite from the bustling mainstream.

Nashville's magic lies not only in its popular attractions but also in the secrets it whispers to those willing to explore beyond the surface. In every alley, around each corner, there's a story waiting to be uncovered, a melody waiting to be heard. As we bid farewell to this journey through Nashville's hot spots and hidden gems, we carry with us the understanding that the soul of the city resides not just in its landmarks but in the collective heartbeat of its people, its history, and its uncharted wonders.

Thank you for sharing in this journey through Nashville. If you would leave a review I would be forever grateful!

Resources

The 28 best things to do when you visit Nashville. (2023, December 8). https://travel.usnews.com/Nashville_TN/Things_To_Do/Day Trips from Nashville -

NAshVILLE, TN Travel Guide: Attractions. (n.d.). 10Best. https://10best.usatoday.com/destinations/tennessee/nashville/attractions/

Fodor's Travel Talk Forums. (n.d.). https://www.fodors.com/community/united-states/day-trips-from-nashville-742559/

OpenAI. (2024). ChatGPT: Conversational AI Language Model. https://www.openai.com/research/chatgpt

Printed in Great Britain
by Amazon